This Little Tiger book
belongs to:

_____

_____

_____

D1341615

C016037843

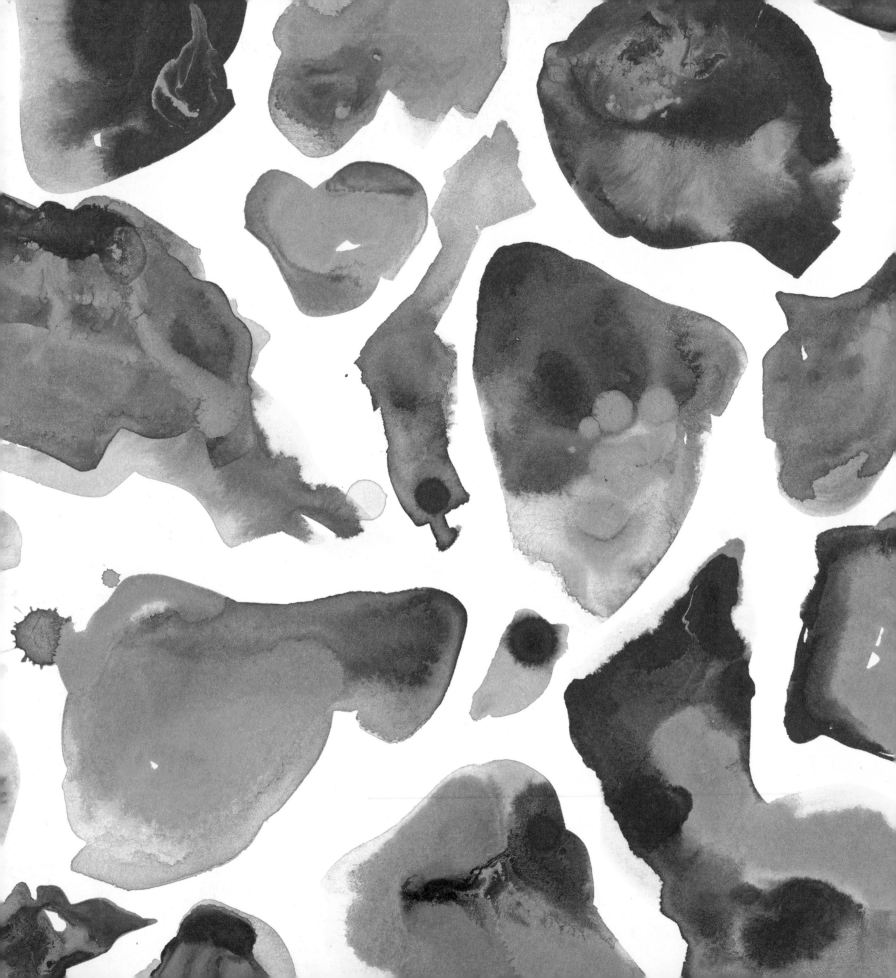

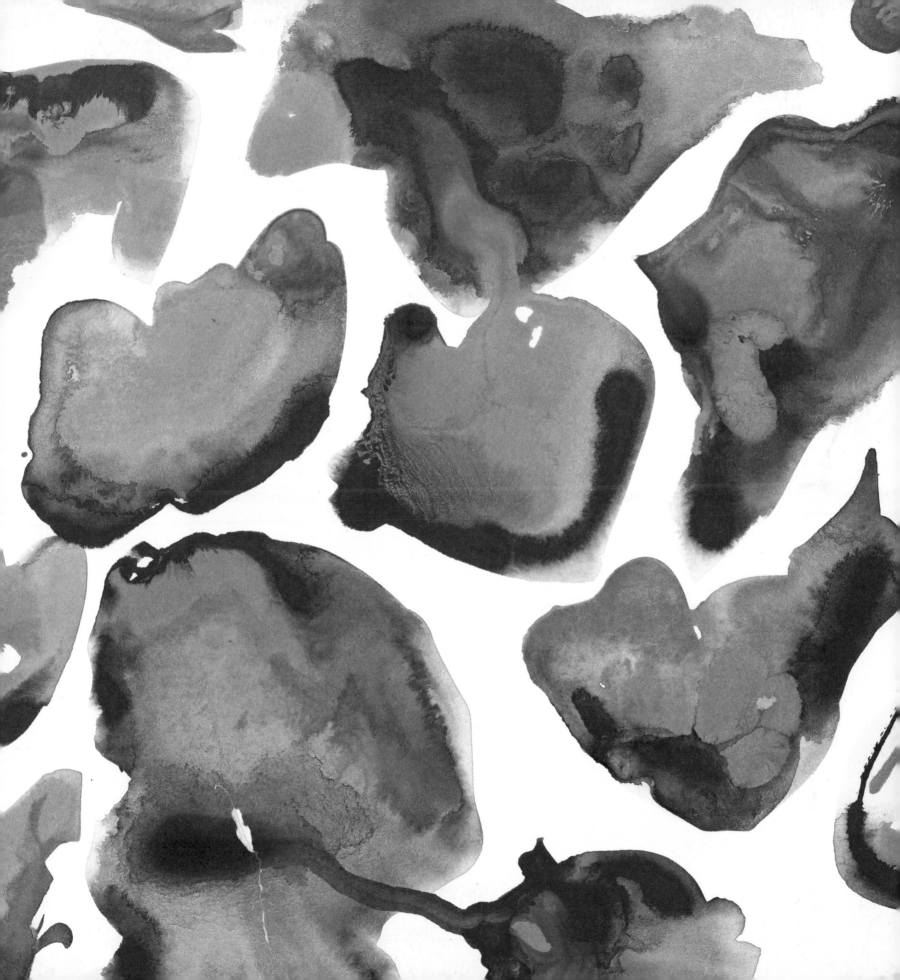

LITTLE TIGER PRESS
1 The Coda Centre, 189 Munster Road, London SW6 6AW
www.littletiger.co.uk • First published in Great Britain 2013 • This edition published 2014
Text and illustrations copyright © Catherine Rayner 2013 • Catherine Rayner has asserted her
right to be identified as the author and illustrator of this work under the Copyright, Designs and
Patents Act, 1988 • A CIP catalogue record for this book is available from the British Library

For Finlay – my little star
C R

ISBN 978-1-84895-646-9
Printed in China • LTP/1800/0762/0514
2 4 6 8 10 9 7 5 3 1

Catherine Rayner

Abigail

LITTLE TIGER PRESS
LONDON

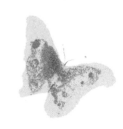

Abigail **loved** to count.
It was her very favourite thing.

She counted the spots on Ladybird.

1
2
3

But Ladybird scuttled
under a leaf.

So Abigail counted the leaves
on the tree.

4 5 6

BUT . . .

. . . somebody was **eating** the leaves!

Crunch!

Munch!

Lunch!

Abigail really wanted to count.
She started counting Zebra's stripes.

7

8

9

"It's INCREDIBLY difficult to count when you are moving, Zebra," grumbled Abigail. But Zebra just couldn't help it.

And there was no point even trying
to count Cheetah's splotches.

Whoosh ...

He was just too fast.

"Come **back**, everybody!" said Abigail, crossly.

"Oh dear," sighed Abigail.
"There must be **something** I can count."

"I know just the thing,"

whispered Ladybird.

"Follow me."

"FLOWERS!" giggled Zebra. "Come on, we'll help you count!"
Unfortunately Abigail's friends were not very good
at counting.

"One . . . two . . . five . . . lots!"

bellowed Zebra.

"One . . . three . . . seven . . . many!"

laughed Cheetah.

It was impossible!

But Abigail was a very patient giraffe.
Carefully she showed her friends
how to count.

1

2

3

4

5

6 7 8 9 10

All day long they practised until at
last their counting was nearly perfect.
But by that time . . .

. . . it was dark.

"Oh no!" grunted Zebra. "How can
we count when the sun has gone?"
Cheetah's tail drooped and Ladybird frowned.

But Abigail just smiled.
"Don't give up, everyone . . ."

"Look!"

High above, the stars were twinkling, and they were not going anywhere . . .

Together, Abigail and her friends counted all night long.

3 friends. 1267 stars.

And 1 Abigail.

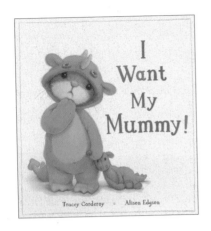

I Want My Mummy!

Tracey Corderoy • Alison Edgson

BIG BAD

STEVE SMALLMAN
RICHARD WATSON

NO!

Tracey Corderoy
Tim Warnes

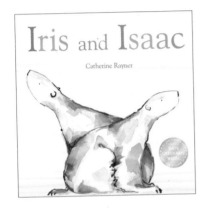

Iris and Isaac

Catherine Rayner

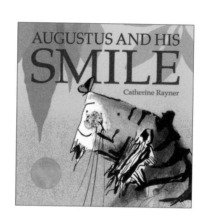

AUGUSTUS AND HIS SMILE

Catherine Rayner

Mighty mo

ALISON BROWN

1 2 3 4 5...

6 amazing books from Little Tiger Press!

For information regarding any of the above titles
or for our catalogue, please contact us:
Little Tiger Press, 1 The Coda Centre,
189 Munster Road, London SW6 6AW
Tel: 020 7385 6333 • Fax: 020 7385 7333
E-mail: contact@littletiger.co.uk • www.littletiger.co.uk